# The SKULL
## Alphabet Book

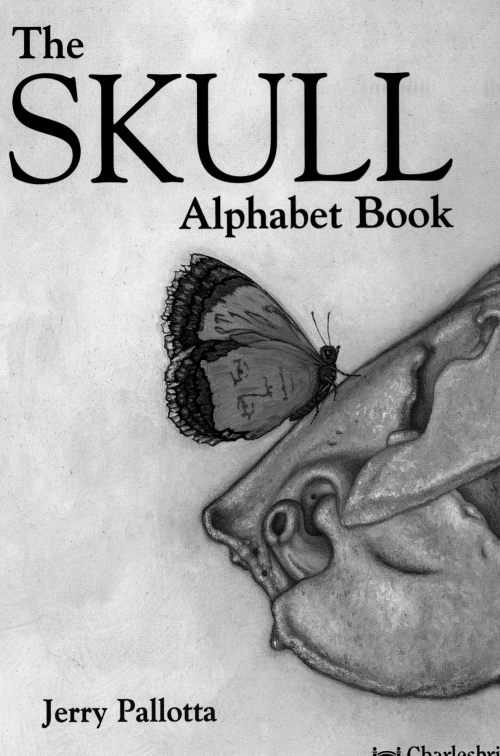

Jerry Pallotta

Ralph Masiello

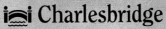
Charlesbridge

This book is dedicated to Jay, Kim, and their children Jay, Josh, Jaron, and Shala.
—Jerry Pallotta

For my little miracle . . . my daughter, Talia.
A special thanks to Stephanie Faucher and Diane Earley for their assistance with the cover design.
—Ralph Masiello

Text copyright © 2002 by Jerry Pallotta
Illustrations copyright © 2002 by Ralph Masiello
All rights reserved, including the right of reproduction
in whole or in part in any form. Charlesbridge and colophon
are registered trademarks of Charlesbridge Publishing, Inc.

Published by Charlesbridge
85 Main Street, Watertown, MA 02472
(617) 926-0329
www.charlesbridge.com

Library of Congress Cataloging-in-Publication Data
Pallotta, Jerry.
   The skull alphabet book/ Jerry Pallotta; illustrated by Ralph Masiello.
      p. cm.
   Summary: Asks the reader to identify, by learning functions of facial bones and
teeth, the skull of an animal for each letter of the alphabet.
   ISBN-13: 978-0-88106-914-3; ISBN-10: 0-88106-914-0 (reinforced for library use)
   ISBN-13: 978-0-88106-915-0; ISBN-10: 0-88106-915-9 (softcover)
1. Skull—Juvenile literature. 2. English language—Alphabet—Juvenile literature.
[1. Skull. 2. Animals—Physiology. 3. Alphabet.] I. Masiello, Ralph, ill. II. Title.
QL821.P18 2002
73.7'6--dc21

                                              2001005932

Printed March 2012 by Sung In Printing in Gunpo-Si, Kyonggi-Do, Korea
(hc) 10 9 8 7 6 5 4
(sc) 10 9 8 7

The answers for this book can be found somewhere in the book.
Look for the presidents of the United States—they are hidden too!

WARNING! This book contains the alphabet. If you are afraid of the alphabet, do not read any further.

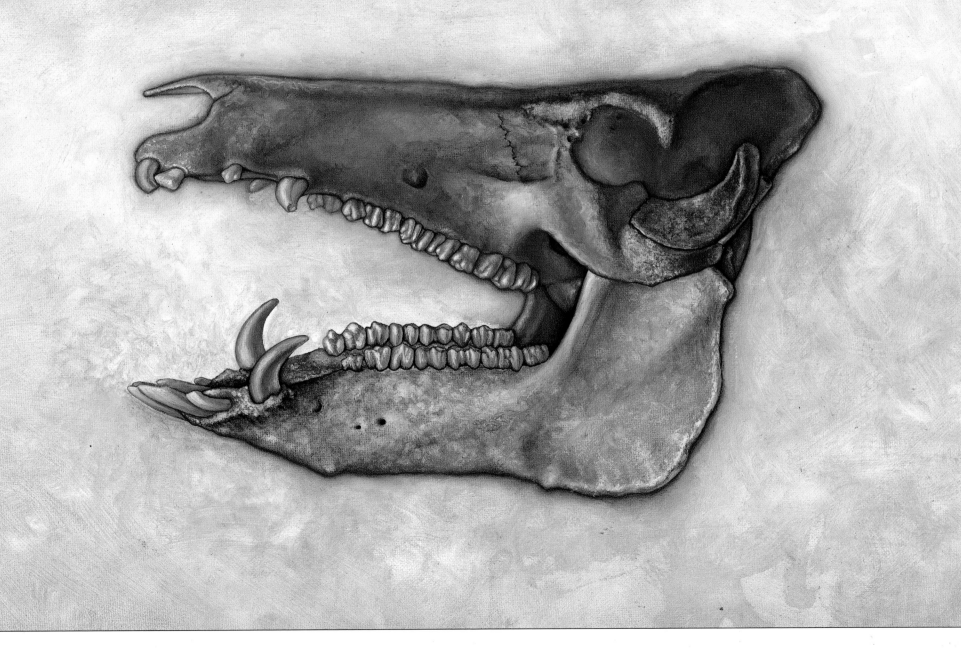

This is a science book about mammal skulls.
A skull is the head of a skeleton. Leg bones,
arm bones, rib bones, and backbones
are not in this book.

# Aa

A is for. . . .
We are not telling you!
As you read this book you will
have to use your skull—actually
what is in your skull: your brain!
Can you guess what animal this is?
Think! Its skull is perfectly shaped for
eating small, six-legged creatures.

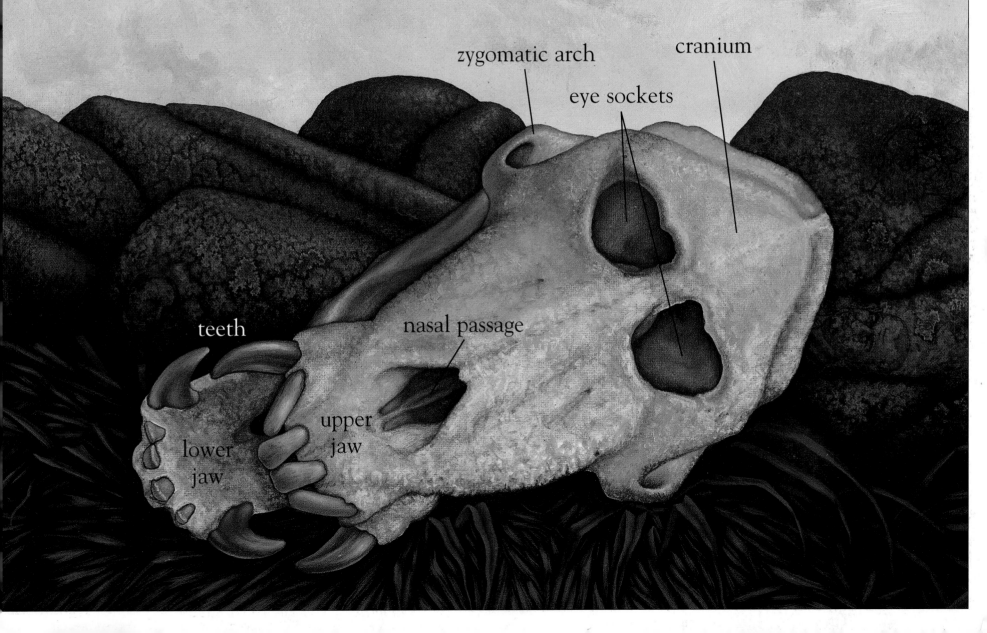

B is for. . . . We are still not telling you! Did you think we were kidding? Every skull tells a story. Be a detective. Look for clues in the different parts of a skull.

Bb

zygomatic arch

cranium

eye sockets

teeth

nasal passage

upper jaw

lower jaw

# Cc

C is for. . . . This skull should be easy to figure out. You do not have to guess; guessing is random. You can figure it out logically! Maybe a warm bowl of milk will help.

# Dd

**D** is for. . . . There are
four different types of teeth:
incisors, canines, bicuspids, and
molars. Canine teeth are sharp and
pointy, perfect for grabbing and holding
food. You can tell this is a meat eater by the
canine teeth. Meat eaters are called carnivores.
There will be no fruits and vegetables for this animal.

# Ee

E is for. . . . The giant sequoia tree is the largest tree on earth. The blue whale is the largest ocean creature. This is the skull of the largest land animal. Its huge molars are flat because it only eats plants.

**F** is for. . . . Brains are mushy. Skulls protect brains. Skulls also protect the organs of four senses: hearing, smell, taste, and sight. A sly person can identify this skull— there are only three letters in its name.

**Ff**

# Gg

G is for. . . . A craniologist is someone who studies skulls. The cranium holds the brain. This animal has a huge skull, but it has a small cranium and therefore a small brain. It cannot read.

**H** is for. . . . Here is the only creature on earth that can read this book! Yay! We all love to read. Notice the huge cranium in relation to the overall size of the skull. If you look in a mirror, you can easily identify this one.

# Hh

# Ii

I is for. . . . This fast and graceful African animal has eye sockets on the sides of its skull. It has monocular vision. Each eye sees something different.

It is always on the lookout because it does not want to get eaten by hungry predators.

**J** is for. . . . Moo! Moo! Mooooooooooooo! This is a cow skull. There are many different types of cows. Do some research: why would a cow be on the "J" page? Cows and other plant eaters are called herbivores.

# Jj

# Kk

K is for. . . . If this marsupial were alive, you would be able to identify it right away. It hops on its hind legs and carries its baby in a pouch. The lower front teeth are very interesting—they are shaped like a trowel.

# Ll

L is for. . . . You can tell this is a predator because the eyes are in the front of its head, looking forward. It has binocular vision just like you. Both eyes look at the same thing. Maybe it is a good time to learn a little poem. "Eyes in front, likes to hunt. Eyes on side, likes to hide."

# Mm

M is for. . . . These animals are experts at climbing and swinging from trees. Scientists have learned that the deoxyribonucleic acid—oh, just call it DNA—of this animal is almost exactly the same as human DNA.

# Nn

N is for. . . . This sea mammal's tusk is one of its teeth that grew extra long. It is sometimes called a swimming unicorn. You are looking at the top of a very different skull. This mammal has a blowhole. Its nasal opening is on top.

# Oo

O is for. . . . This is the only great ape that lives in Asia. It spends almost its whole life in trees. You can clearly see the jaws. The upper jaw is called the maxilla. The lower jaw is called the mandible.

**P** is for. . . . This skull is very unusual. It has carnivore-type teeth, but the animal only eats bamboo. You can look right into the nasal passage and see where the sinuses were.

Pp

# Qq

Q is for. . . . Right away, we will tell you that this is a porcupine skull. It is often called something else. Do some more research; figure it out!

It is easy to see the zygomatic arches. They were connected to muscles that moved the jaw.

# Rr

R is for. . . . Here is a skull
with two horns. What is the
difference between a horn
and an antler? Horns stay
attached to the skull, while
antlers are shed every year.
The white-tailed deer on
the front cover of this book
has antlers.

# Ss

S is for. . . . The bumblebee bat of Thailand is considered the smallest mammal on earth. This is the skull of the smallest mammal in North America. Its skull is less than an inch long. This creature eats bugs. Bug eaters are called insectivores.

**T** is for. . . . It is not a lion or a bear. Oh my!
This ferocious carnivore is the largest cat in
the world. If you see one of these, *RUN*,
but it can run faster than you.

**Tt**

# Uu

U is for. . . . It is unknown. The government denies the existence of these aliens. What planet are they from? It is unknown. What language did they speak? It is unknown. What material are their skulls made of? It is unknown. If someone asks you about this unidentified flying skull say: "I don't know anything!"

WELCOME TO ROSWELL

**V** is for. . . . Does this page make you
wonder what type of blood you have?
This flying mammal is nocturnal.
Nocturnal animals come out at night.
This animal has a bad reputation,
but it has very tiny teeth.
Do not be afraid.

Vv

In Memory of

And now, an alphabet break.
Here are some nonmammal skulls:
a crocodile, a fish, a tuatara, a
salamander, two birds, and a turtle.

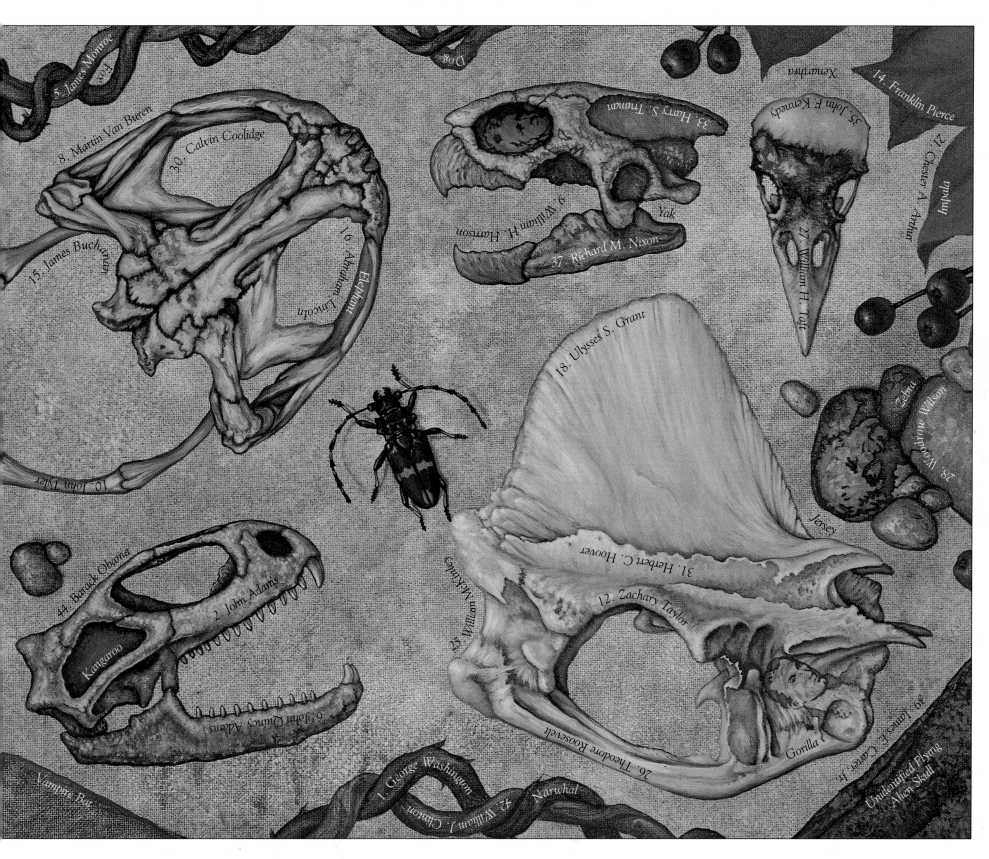

# Ww

W is for. . . . This animal is a member of the pig family. It eats everything. Herbivores eat plants. Carnivores eat meat. Insectivores eat bugs. Animals that eat everything are called omnivores. People eat everything too! After reading this book, you can go eat some bugs!

Scientists classify animals like this: kingdom, phylum, class, order, family, genus, and species.

X is for armadillo. That's right! Armadillo! Why? Because it is from the animal kingdom, phylum Chordata, class Mammalia, order Xenarthra, family Dasypodidae, genus *Dasypus*, species *novemcinctus*. It is a nine-banded armadillo, which is in the same order with sloths, anteaters, and other armadillos.

# Y y

Y is for. . . . This hairy animal lives in high altitudes and subzero weather. The female is called a nak!

Skulls are not just one piece of solid bone. The many parts are held together by jagged joints called sutures.

Ignore the vulture.

**Z** is not for zebra shark, zebra mussel, zebra swallowtail butterfly, zebra moray eel, zebra grass, zebra pipefish, zebra finch, zebra caterpillar, zebra-tailed lizard, zebra spider, or zebra worm. In a zillion tries can you figure it out?
**Z** is for . . .

**Z z**

Thank you, Jay Villemarette of Skulls Unlimited International, Inc., for generously loaning us every skull in this book. The skull alphabet is over, but here's one more: Jay's favorite skull. The babirusa is a wild pig from the island of Sulawesi. See more skulls at www.skullsunlimited.com.